OZZY'S ADVENTURE

Kelsey Sweetland

AUTHOR AND ILLUSTRATOR

SAVE THE
⇉ MONARCH BUTTERFLIES! ⇇

The monarch butterfly is known for one of the most incredible insect migrations on Earth. The western monarch migrates 300 miles from Colorado to California, and the eastern monarch travels an astounding 3000 miles from upper Canada to central Mexico. In the 1990s there were 1.2 million monarchs. But that is not the case today.

Pesticides, global warming, and the loss of their only food source, milkweed, have nearly driven the monarchs to extinction. The eastern monarch population has fallen 80% since the 1990s, and in 2020 the western monarch population declined to fewer than 2000 butterflies! Monarch butterflies heavily rely on milkweed because it is the only food monarch caterpillars can eat. Without milkweed, monarch caterpillars will starve to death. A large portion of milkweed is disappearing because of chemical weed killers like Roundup and pesticides. Many monarchs use agricultural fields with milkweed as key spots in their migration, but when farmers use pesticides and herbicides, it kills the milkweed in and around the fields. The loss of milkweed may be the largest contributing factor to the monarch's decline.

Pollinators like monarchs are a critical part of our ecosystem. Monarch butterflies pollinate plants, which create fruit and seeds that many animals rely on – including humans. The Nature Conservancy estimates that one out of every three bites of food we eat exists because of pollinators like monarchs.

In 2020, the U.S. Fish and Wildlife Service proposed that Monarch butterflies should be listed on the endangered species list. Being on this list would allow monarch butterflies to have government support so they can begin to recover. Unfortunately, Monarch butterflies were denied that label in 2020 despite meeting the endangered species criteria. When the endangered species list is updated in 2024, monarch butterflies need to be put on this list so they can gain recognition and support. Otherwise, they may never recover.

We still have time to save the monarch butterflies. Here are some things you can do to help:

1. Plant native milkweed
2. Avoid using pesticides and herbicides in your garden
3. Buy organic food
4. Create a Monarch Waystation (www.MonarchWatch.org/ws)
5. Ask Congress to pass the MONARCH Act of 2021 (xerces.org/monarch-act has an easy-to-use draft letter to send to your senators and representatives).
6. Learn more (saveourmonarchs. org is a great resource)
7. Spread the word!

Every person makes a difference in this crisis. If we take action now hopefully we can see monarch populations recover and have these extraordinary creatures return to our forests, gardens, and skies once again.

My name is Ozzy. I live on a farm, and I love to chase BUTTERFLIES!

On a beautiful spring morning I sit down on my favorite railing and sniff the fresh air. Then sitting on a flower I see...

a BUTTERFLY.

I must **catch** it!

I CROUCH,

I POUNCE,

and... I MISS.

I must chase the BUTTERFLY!

With my stealthy feet,
I follow the butterfly
off the PORCH,

into the FIELD,

past the BARN,

until the FOREST. Do I follow?

YES I will!

I chase the crafty butterfly through TREES,

under LOGS,

around MUSHROOMS,

until a STREAM.

Do I follow?

YES I will!

I chase the sneaky
butterfly over LEAVES,

between ROCKS,   through PLANTS,

until a CAVE.

Do I follow?

YES I will!

I chase the tricky BUTTERFLY out of the cave,

then up a GRASSY hill.

The BUTTERFLY spirals high above me
then softly lands on
my NOSE.

After a moment the BUTTERFLY flutters away.

Should I follow?

No, it is time for Ozzy to go home.

Goodbye BUTTERFLY.

I go home and fall asleep,

dreaming about the butterfly and

our ADVENTURE.

The next MORNING I sit down in my regular spot when I see...

The BUTTERFLY!

Another DAY, another ADVENTURE.

÷ ABOUT THE AUTHOR ÷

Kelsey Sweetland is 15 years old and lives with her mom, dad, brother, and cat in California. Kelsey loves the outdoors and is a passionate protector of nature. This is Kelsey's third book. She donates a portion of each purchase to organizations that protect animals and their habitats. In *Ozzy's Adventure* she donates to non-profits who protect the monarch butterflies. You can find Kelsey's other books, *Natalie the Narwhal* and *Elliot the Egret* on Amazon!

Follow Kelsey on Instagram!

KELSEYSWEETLANDPUBLISHING

CPSIA information can be obtained
at www.ICGtesting.com
Printed in the USA
BVHW020024270522
637876BV00002B/9

* 9 7 8 1 0 8 7 9 2 4 2 9 8 *